W9-CMB-705

Lois B. Hart, Ed.D.

Saying Goodbye:

Ending a
Group Experience

**Organization Design
and Development, Inc.**
King of Prussia, Pennsylvania

Copyright 1983, 1989 by Lois B. Hart

All rights reserved. No part of this book may be reproduced, stored in a retrieval system, or transmitted in whole or in part, in any form or by any means, electronic, mechanical, photocopying, recording, or otherwise, without the prior written permission of Organization Design and Development, Inc., 2002 Renaissance Boulevard, Suite 100, King of Prussia, PA 19406. (215) 279-2002.

Prepared for publication by Organization Design and Development, Inc. Printed in the United States of America.

First Printing: 1983
Second Printing: 1987
Second Edition: 1989

Library of Congress Catalog Card Number: 89-60504

ISBN: 0-925652-05-9

Contents

Preface

While I was working on *Saying Hello: Getting Your Group Started*, a resource book of warm-up activities, I recognized that there was the same need for a companion book of activities that would help trainers and group leaders close their programs.

Saying Goodbye: Ending a Group Experience was originally published in 1983 and reprinted twice through my company, Leadership Dynamics. Rollin Glaser, president of Organization Design and Development, recognized its potential and offered to publish it in a new updated edition. We are proud of this new book and know you will find it useful in your work.

Several of my professional colleagues have made contributions to this book or have made suggestions for varying some of the activities I had already included. I am grateful to the following creative people: Rollin Glaser, Dr. Marshall Sashkin, Dr. Joel Goodman, Dr. John E. Jones, Dr. Sidney Simon, and Dr. Jerry Weinstein.

All of these activities have been tested many times with thousands of people. If you have an activity that consistently works for you, or a creative variation on one found in this book, send it to me for possible inclusion in a future edition of *Saying Goodbye*.

Lois B. Hart, Ed.D.
Boulder, Colorado

Foreword

One of the most significant of the many contributions to the field of human resource development made by Bill Pfeiffer and John Jones was figuring out a way to share training activities with others in the field. Some of us still remember their first publication, a four inch by six inch spiral-bound "handbook" containing two dozen "structured experiences for human relations training." Since then there have been many handbooks, from a variety of sources. Some have been great, a few not so great, and almost all have contained at least some useful "exercises" for use in training and HRD.

There remains, however, a problem, despite this apparent abundance of training resources. Very few of the many resources now available — thanks to John's and Bill's innovation — focus on a single topic or theme; most are compilations of miscellaneous activities that cut across a wide range of topics. When we saw the earlier editions of Lois Hart's books, *Saying Hello* and *Saying Goodbye*, we knew immediately that here was a training resource that really filled an unmet need.

One of the more difficult parts of a training design — and of conducting a training activity — is concluding the event so that good closure is achieved. It is not just that we all feel more comfortable when we sense a clear "finish" that wraps up things neatly. Nor is it simply that what participants learn is reinforced when they have a chance to see and feel their accomplishments. The purpose of most training is to give participants something that they can apply, some skills or knowledge that will be useful to them "back home." When a seminar, workshop, or training event ends with the participants feeling a sense of completion and accomplishment, they will be more likely to go back to their "real" lives ready to apply what they have learned.

For this reason, we feel that Lois Hart's structured exercises for wrapping up, closing, and ending group activities will be an important and valuable resource for HRD trainers and consultants. Lois has put together a collection of outstanding exercises, based on her extensive experience as a trainer and HRD practitioner and drawing on the ideas of her colleagues. The first edition of this collection, a careful distillation of exceptionally effective activities, was an outstanding product.

We asked Lois to revise that first edition, taking into account her own experiences since it was first published. We each contributed a few new structured exercises that we have used and found to be especially effective.

The new, revised edition of *Saying Goodbye* contains 40 structured exercises. Most experienced trainers probably will be familiar with at least a few of these, but we doubt that anyone will have run across most — or even many — of them. Lois has retained her original classification scheme, which enables users to "fine tune" their designs and focus on or deal with the specific wrap-up issues of a particular training group. We have enjoyed helping with this revision. We feel both a sense of closure and accomplishment, and we hope that you will find in this book the kind of training resources that are applicable to your own issues and concerns when you "say goodbye."

Rollin Glaser
Marshall Sashkin
John E. Jones

Introduction

"Saying Goodbye" is just the other side of "Saying Hello!" Planning how you will end your workshop or program is as important as the other components of your program design—yet too often this crucial step is glossed over or ignored.

Participants need an opportunity to express their feelings toward one another, to reflect upon what they have just experienced, and to plan what they will take from the experience back to their work and personal lives.

Saying Goodbye: Ending a Group Experience was written for planners of educational and training programs, meetings, and conferences. All of these events have to end in some way, therefore, you might as well do it creatively and meaningfully.

You will notice that the word "facilitator" is used throughout the book to represent the various roles of a group leader, trainer, educator, meeting leader, teacher, instructor, or seminar leader.

The farewell rituals and ideas in *Saying Goodbye* are written to help participants take the best from your training program. The inclusion of one or more of these activities in your training design should help participants apply what they have learned and perhaps be more ready to "say hello" to your next training program.

Here are the recommended steps to follow for selecting the most appropriate activity for your workshop or conference:

1. Identify the goals and objectives for your entire program. Once you have these stated, you can more easily select the best activities from this book.

   For example, if the program will run more than one day you will want to include a closing activity that will allow time for participants to share their perceptions of one another.

2. Determine what you know about your participants. How many people will be attending? Will there be enough time for them to learn enough about one another during the workshop?

3. Determine how much time you can allot for an ending activity.

   Each activity in this book indicates the approximate time required. Once you have selected an activity, leave enough time in your design for participants to complete that activity effectively.

4. The matrix that follows this introduction is a handy reference for comparing the activities relative to their primary purpose, how many participants can be involved, and how much time is needed.

   For example, if you need an activity that will end a one-half day program involving thirty people, but you can only allot fifteen minutes, look down the appropriate columns listing these variables until you find the most appropriate activity.

5. Next, keeping your goals, program design, and participants in mind, review the activities from the most appropriate chapter.

   Each activity lists its objectives, optimal group size, time needed, room set-up, supplies and equipment requirements, step-by-step instructions for facilitating the activity, and variations you could try.

   Remember, a given activity might not fit your needs exactly, so adapt, modify, mix, and match the activities.

6. After you use an activity, be sure to make notes on what you actually did, how it worked, and ideas for improvements for future use.

There are seven chapters in this book. Here is a brief description of each one:

I. **Looking Back and Planning Ahead**	These activities summarize the objectives of your workshop, review the skills and content covered, check on the participants' original expectations, and provide an opportunity for setting goals and developing action plans.
II. **Sharing Positive Feedback**	These activities help participants to focus on each other and work on giving positive feedback.
III. **Giving Prizes, Gifts, and Awards**	These activities outline some fun prizes, awards or creative certificates that can be given to the participants.
IV. **Coming Home**	These activities help the participants prepare for their re-entry back at work or home.
V. **Staying in Touch**	These activities cover ways that the participants can stay in contact with one another following the workshop or program.
VI. **Saying Goodbye**	These short activities include ways to say goodbye nonverbally, plus some quick closing ceremonies.
VII. **Following Up**	These activities can be used following your workshop so that participants receive additional ideas and reinforcement of what you presented during your program.

You could enhance this book by adding other activities you have used in the past. Label them with the appropriate chapter, add them to your Table of Contents, and create an additional matrix for future reference.

Activity	Chapter							Group Size						Time				
	1	2	3	4	5	6	7	10	20	30	40	50	Any	15	30	45	60	+

Looking Back and Planning Ahead

Activity	1	2	3	4	5	6	7	10	20	30	40	50	Any	15	30	45	60	+
Reflect and Share	●							●	●	●				●	●	●		
My Personal Learning Goal	●							●	●	●				●				
I Learned and Plan To . . .	●							●	●					●	●			
Peaks and Valleys	●							●	●					●	●			
Summing Up	●												●	●				
Looking Back and Planning Ahead	●												●	●				
Self Contract	●												●	●	●			
Dear Boss	●												●	●				
Setting . . . Goals	●												●		●			
The Action Plan	●												●	●	●			
Evaluating Goals	●												●	●	●			
Step by Step to Action	●												●		●			
Goal Rehearsal . . .	●												●	●	●			

Sharing Positive Feedback

Activity	1	2	3	4	5	6	7	10	20	30	40	50	Any	15	30	45	60	+
Stroke Collection		●						●	●	●				●				
Golden Star Awards		●							●	●	●			●				
Stickers		●						●	●					●				
The Gift		●						●	●					●	●			
Thank You For . . .		●											●	●				
We Saw You As . . .		●						●	●					●	●			
Appreciation Circle		●						●	●					●	●	●		
Card Line-Up		●						●	●						●	●		

Giving Prizes, Gifts, and Awards

Activity	1	2	3	4	5	6	7	10	20	30	40	50	Any	15	30	45	60	+
Door Prizes			●					●	●					●	●			
The Certificate of Participation			●					●	●	●				●				
The Certificate of Appreciation			●						●	●	●				●			
The Certificate of Self-Appreciation			●						●	●	●			●				
Team Awards			●										●				●	●

Activity	Chapter							Group Size						Time				
	1	2	3	4	5	6	7	10	20	30	40	50	Any	15	30	45	60	+
Coming Home																		
The Re-Entry				•									•	•				
Hi! I'm Home!				•				•	•	•					•	•	•	
Staying in Touch																		
The Name Exchange					•								•		•			
The Postcard					•								•	•				
Support Groups					•								•		•			
Saying Goodbye																		
The Closing Circle						•		•	•					•				
The Wiggle Handshake						•							•	•				
The Circle Massage						•		•	•					•				
Exclamations!						•							•	•				
Final Words						•							•	•				
Let's Sing!						•							•	•				
Following Up																		
You'll Be Hearing From Me							•						•				•	
Success is Up to You!							•						•				•	
A Letter to Myself							•						•	•	•			

1

Looking Back
and Planning Ahead

The activities in this first chapter provide an opportunity to summarize the objectives of the workshop and review the skills and content covered. The participants can also compare their original expectations with what they have gained from the learning experience.

Several variations of goal setting and developing action plans are included.

Reflect and Share

Objectives   To compare quickly the participants' expectations with what they actually have gained from the workshop

Group Size   Up to twenty-five participants per facilitator is best; could be used without a facilitator in small groups of eight to ten

Time Required   One to three minutes per participant

Physical Setting   Circle of chairs

Materials Utilized   None

Content and Process

1. Remind participants that they each had stated their expectations at the beginning of the workshop. (These might have been posted on a flip chart at the beginning of the session.) Ask them to review silently the expectations they stated or wrote earlier and then compare those expectations with what they actually gained from the experience.

2. Starting with the facilitator, each person completes the sentence stem, "My expectation for the workshop was . . ."   "What I gained was . . ."

3. Do not ask for explanations. Allow people to pass if they do not want to share this information with the group.

4. Summarize what you have heard from the participants and share your general impressions of them as a group.

Variations / Comments   Other sentence stems you could use are:

"I plan to take from this experience . . ."

"I had hoped that we would discuss . . ."

Notes to Myself

My Personal Learning Goal

Objectives

To set learning goals for the program

To evaluate how effectively / successfully the goals were reached

Group Size

Up to thirty participants

Time Required

Fifteen to twenty minutes

Physical Setting

Any setting

Materials Utilized

Flip chart and markers

Content and Process

1. At the beginning of the session, ask participants to think about what goals they want to achieve as a result of the program.

2. One by one ask participants to stand and state one of their learning goals. Record the goals on flip chart paper with the heading "Personal Learning Goals."

3. Post the sheets of paper on the walls of the meeting room for the remainder of the program. These sheets will serve as a reminder to participants of the goals they have set for themselves.

4. At the end of the session, tell the participants that you would like them to tell the group 1) what their goal was, 2) how successful they were in reaching their goal, on a scale of one to five, 3) reasons why they did or did not reach their goal, and 4) whether or not they were satisfied with the goal they set for themselves and why (or why not). Give participants a few moments to prepare their thoughts.

Notes to Myself

I Learned and Plan To . . .

Objectives To review topics covered in the workshop

To identify what participants learned about themselves

Group Size Up to twenty; if more, form small groups of six to eight participants

Time Required Fifteen to thirty minutes

Physical Setting Tables and chairs

Materials Utilized Handout — "I Learned . . ."

Content and Process

1. Prepare a handout like the sample shown below. Have these printed on 3" x 5" (or 4" x 6") cards.

I learned that I _____

I re-learned that I _____

I discovered that I _____

I noticed that I _____

I was surprised that I _____

I am disappointed that I _____

I plan to _____

---

2. Distribute one card per participant. Explain the importance of evaluating what was learned in the workshop. Point out that learning is personal, therefore they will be asked to reflect upon what they learned about themselves.

3. Ask the participants to complete several (or all) of the sentence stems listed on the card. They have to complete the first and last stems listed (learned . . . , plan to . . .).

4. Ask for participants to share some of their statements. (If there are more than twenty people, divide them into groups of six to eight for sharing.) Do not elaborate on what they say. Thank each person who shares with the group.

Variations / Tie the "I Learned . . . " statements into goal setting
Comments activities such as those found later in this chapter.

Notes to Myself

Peaks and Valleys

Objectives   To review topics covered in the workshop

To identify the highs and lows of the experience

Group Size   Up to twenty participants; if more, sharing can be done in small groups

Time Required   Fifteen to thirty minutes

Physical Setting   Tables and chairs

Materials Utilized   Handout — "Peaks and Valleys"

Content and Process

1. Prepare a handout like the one that follows. It could be modified by listing your original objectives / topics, plus the name of your workshop.

2. Distribute one handout per participant. Explain the importance of reflecting on their experiences in the workshop, focusing on the best part of the experience and the parts that were disappointing. Use the analogy of mountain top highs (peak experiences) and accompanying valleys (disappointing experiences) as shown graphically on the handout.

3. Ask the participants to write in several of their high and low experiences.

4. Ask participants to share one of their highs and lows. (If there are more than twenty people, divide them into groups of six to eight for sharing.) Do not elaborate on what they say. If shared with the total group, thank each person who shares.

Notes to Myself

My Peaks and Valleys

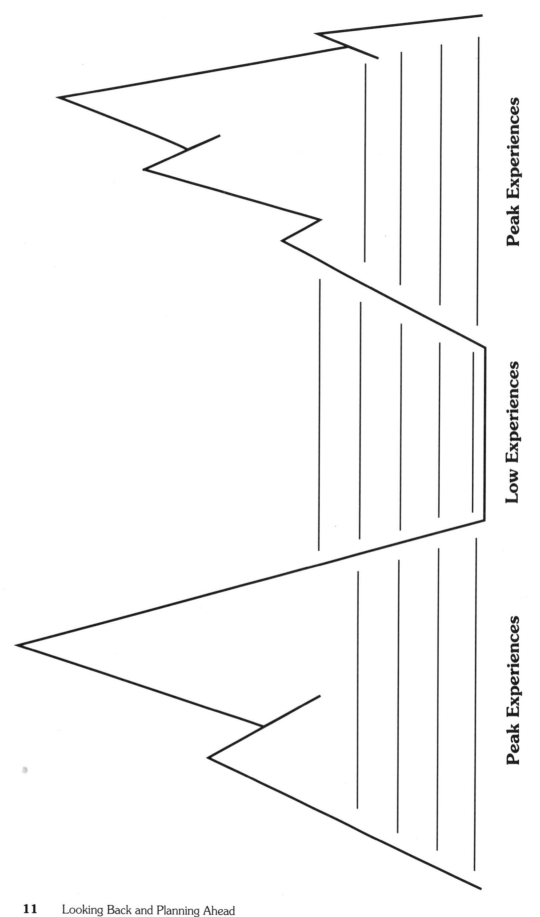

Peak Experiences

Low Experiences

Peak Experiences

Notes to Myself

Summing Up

Objectives   To summarize workshop topics and objectives

To provide time for additional questions

To identify additional resources

Group Size   Any size

Time Required   Ten to fifteen minutes

Physical Setting   Chairs facing the front of the room

Materials Utilized   Flip chart, markers; or copies of workshop topics /
objectives handout if it was provided prior to the workshop

Content and Process

1. Draw attention to either the flip chart listing or handout
   that outlined the objectives / topics of your workshop.

2. If they were posted on the flip chart, use one colored
   marker to check off those objectives / topics that you
   covered during the workshop. Allow time for additional
   questions and answers.

3. With a second color, star those objectives / topics that
   you were unable to cover and explain why (lack of time,
   lower priority, you were not prepared). Identify resources that could help meet these objectives.

4. If using the handout, ask the participants to make the
   appropriate marks on their copy.

Notes to Myself

Looking Back and Planning Ahead

Objectives   To review topics covered in the workshop

To identify topics that participants will actually apply

To set one goal

Group Size   Any size

Time Required   Ten to fifteen minutes

Physical Setting   Tables and chairs

Materials Utilized   Handout — "Looking Back and Planning Ahead"

Content and Process

1. Prepare a handout like the example that follows to fit your workshop topic. Note that Section A is a list of topics and issues of the program, worded as potential goals.

2. Distribute one copy of the handout per participant. Explain the importance of evaluating their experiences in the workshop so that each can focus on the most important areas they can apply to their own lives. Clarify the directions that are written on the handout and ask them to complete parts A and B.

3. Explain the importance of sharing their goal(s) with another person who can encourage them when needed, help them to think of alternative strategies for accomplishing the goal, and with whom they can celebrate when the goal is accomplished. Suggest they either select a person from the workshop group or another individual in their lives who will "witness" their goal statement.

4. Ask for volunteers who would like to share their goal with the rest of the group.

**Variations /
Comments**
See the activity "Self-Contract" that appears later in the
chapter.

Notes to Myself

Looking Back and Planning Ahead

A. Read over the following list of topics and issues we have covered in this program. Put a check mark next to each one you especially need to apply to your life. Add your own topics on the blank lines.

_____ Diagnose future miscommunications using the cycle and checklist
_____ Check out my perceptions of others
_____ Use one way vs. two way communication more appropriately
_____ Check out assumptions more thoroughly
_____ Reduce my defensiveness
_____ Apply the three listening skills
_____ Practice giving and receiving negative feedback
_____ Incorporate more positive feedback in my communication
_____ Value myself more
_____ Disclose more of myself in the right situations
_____ Increase my awareness of how both I and others communicate nonverbally
_____ Plan more carefully how I communicate directions
_____ Ask better questions
_____ Communicate more assertively
_____ Discuss what I have learned with _____
_____ Read or learn more about communication

_____

_____

B. Rank each topic or issue that has a check mark by it. Put a "1" next to the topic you most need to develop, a "2" next to the second most important one, and so forth.

C. Select one area that you will work on immediately and complete the following:

I, _____ , will try to achieve the goal of _____

_____ .

The *first step* I will take is _____ .

My target date for *accomplishing* my goal is _____ .

Date _____   Signed _____

Witnessed by _____

Notes to Myself

Self Contract

Objectives To make a contract with oneself to change a behavior or attitude or to apply a particular skill

Group Size Any size

Time Required Fifteen to thirty minutes

Physical Setting Tables and chairs

Materials Utilized Self Contract cards — 4" x 6"

Content and Process

1. Prepare "Self Contract" cards like the sample shown below.

Self Contract

I, _____ , will try to achieve the goal of _____
_____ . The first step I will take is
_____ .
My target date for reaching my goal is _____ .

Date _____ Signed _____
Witness _____

---

2. Explain the importance of applying what was learned in the workshop to one's life. We often set too many goals for ourselves; therefore, it is better to select the most important one and work only on that goal.

3. Distribute the "Self Contract" cards. Ask the participants to think about their goals for applying what they have learned in this workshop. They should select one goal and complete the Self Contract.

4. Individuals decide who will witness the signing of their contract and obtain that signature. The witness gets a copy of the contract, is committed to reviewing the individual's progress, and generally is to lend support to the change effort. They may even meet upon completion of the goal to "burn the contract"!

5. Sample goals can be shared voluntarily with the total group.

Variations / Comments

Give participants a postcard on which they write out their goal. When the goal is reached, the postcard should be mailed to the "witness" and / or the facilitator.

Notes to Myself

Dear Boss

Objectives

To review the topics covered in the workshop

To identify topics that participants will actually apply

To inform one's boss about what was accomplished in the workshop

Group Size

Any size

Time Required

Ten to fifteen minutes

Physical Setting

Tables and chairs

Materials Utilized

Paper (8-1/2" x 11") and envelopes

Content and Process

1. Explain the importance of reflecting on their experiences in the workshop so they can focus on the most important areas that they can apply to their lives. Discuss reasons why their bosses let them come or sent them to this workshop and the value of communicating to the boss what was learned.

2. Pass out the paper and envelopes. Ask them each to compose a letter to their boss. Include in the letter:

   a. the most important skills, concepts, or issues they have learned

   b. specific behavior or skills they plan to implement upon returning to work

   c. additional training they feel they need to do their job better

   d. an expression of appreciation for time off to attend the workshop.

3. Ask for volunteers to share highlights of their letters.

Variations /
Comments
Have the participants write the letter to a spouse or friend. This variation is especially helpful when participants have been away from home for several days to attend the program.

Notes to Myself

Setting Personal, Interpersonal, and Organizational Goals

Objectives   To identify three types of change: personal, interpersonal, and organizational

Group Size   Any size

Time Required   Thirty minutes

Physical Setting   Tables and chairs

Materials Utilized   Handout — "Setting Personal, Interpersonal, and Organizational Goals"

Content and Process
1. Prepare a handout like the one that follows.

2. Distribute a copy of the handout to each participant. Explain the importance of applying what was learned in the workshop to one's life.

3. Ask the participants to list one goal they have for changing themselves (personal), one relationship they want to change (interpersonal), and one change at work they would like to make (organizational). For each change, they should describe the situation that currently exists and the desired change. Then they should determine what might result if the change occurred and what the results will be if it does not.

4. In triads, each person reviews his/her three goals. The other group members make suggestions, ask clarifying questions, and generally lend support to the individual's plans to change.

5. Sample goals can be shared voluntarily with the entire group.

Variations / Comments   Participants could develop more specific plans using the activity "Step by Step to Action" found in this chapter.

Notes to Myself

Setting Personal, Interpersonal, and Organizational Goals

Type of Change	Current Situation	Desired Change(s)	Results if Change Occurs	Results if Change Does Not Occur
Personal				
Interpersonal				
Organizational				

Notes to Myself

The Action Plan

Objectives   To ensure that a plan of action follows the learning experience

Group Size   Any size

Time Required   Fifteen to thirty minutes

Physical Setting   Tables and chairs

Materials Utilized   Handout — "The Action Plan"

Content and Process

1. Prepare a handout like the sample that follows.

2. Distribute one copy of the handout to each participant. Explain the importance of applying what was learned in the workshop to one's life.

3. Review the five criteria for setting a goal as listed on the handout. Give some examples of each criterion.

4. Ask them to review silently what they have learned during the workshop. You may want to remind them of the topics you have covered.

5. Participants then select one area in which they would like to apply what they have learned and complete the remainder of the handout.

6. In triads, each person reviews his/her plan for action. The other group members make suggestions, ask clarifying questions, and generally lend support to the individual's plans to change.

7. Sample plans can be shared voluntarily with the entire group.

**Variations /
Comments**

- Participants could develop more specific plans using the activities "Evaluating Goals" or "Step by Step to Action" found in this chapter.

- Arrange for a "reunion" so the group members can share their progress and celebrate their accomplishments.

Notes to Myself

The Action Plan for _____
(name)

Success in daily living can be enhanced by action — talking about "what I want to do" and doing it are two different things. Goal setting is a means to action. Some criteria for useful goals include the following:

1.	Conceivable:	Means capable of being put into words.
2.	Achievable:	Means it is realistic given your strengths, abilities, and situation.
3.	Valuable:	Means it is acceptable and desirable according to your values.
4.	Tackle-able:	Means you deal with only one goal at a time.
5.	Growth Facilitating:	Means it does not harm you, others, or society.

1. My goal will be: _____

_____

2. This goal will be accomplished by: _____

_____

3. How important is it to me to reach this goal? What would happen if I reached my goal? _____

_____

What would happen if I did not reach my goal? _____

_____

4. What personal strengths and resources do I have that will help me reach my goal?

_____

5. What other personal strengths or resources will be needed to reach my goal?

_____

6. What will keep me from reaching my goal? _____

_____

7. What will I do to celebrate the reaching of my goal? _____

_____

Notes to Myself

Evaluating Goals

Objectives
To evaluate the value of stated goals

Group Size
Any size

Time Required
Fifteen to thirty minutes

Physical Setting
Tables and chairs

Materials Utilized
Handout — "Evaluating My Goals"

Content and Process

1. Prepare a handout like the one that follows.

2. Distribute one copy of the handout per participant. Explain the importance of applying what was learned in the workshop to one's life. Indicate that we need to select goals that are useful as well as important to us.

3. Ask the participants to list up to four goals they have for applying what they have learned in the workshop.

4. Next, they should weigh each goal against the list of eight statements on the handout, checking off those that apply.

5. In triads, each person reviews his/her goals and observations about their value. The other group members make suggestions, ask clarifying questions, and generally lend support to the individual's plans to change.

6. Sample goals can be shared voluntarily with the entire group.

Variations / Comments
Participants could develop more specific plans using the activity "Step by Step to Action" found in this chapter.

Notes to Myself

Evaluating My Goals

My Goals	1. To make five new sales contacts each day.	2.	3.	4.	
1. This goal is very important to me.	✔				
2. I am proud that it is a goal of mine.					
3. It is realistic in that I have a good chance of achieving the goal.	✔				
4. I have chosen this goal because I want to work toward it, not just because others want me to do it.	✔				
5. There are risks or possible negative consequences involved in achieving this goal.					
6. I have weighed the risks involved and still think the goal is worth it.					
7. This goal is consistent with the other goals I have set for myself.					
8. I am going to make a plan of action to achieve this goal.	✔				

Notes to Myself

Step by Step to Action

Objectives

To list the steps necessary to accomplish a goal

To identify both barriers and helping variables in accomplishing each step

Group Size

Any size

Time Required

Thirty minutes

Physical Setting

Tables and chairs

Materials Utilized

Handout — "Step by Step to Action"

Content and Process

1. Prepare a handout like the one that follows.

2. Distribute one copy of the handout per participant. Explain the importance of identifying the specific steps necessary to reach a stated goal successfully.

3. Ask the participants to list one goal they have for applying what they have learned in the workshop and the date by which they hope to complete it.

4. Next, the participants should list the steps needed to accomplish this goal. To the right of each step, list both the barriers or difficulties they might have to face plus those resources available to help them accomplish their goal.

5. In triads, each person reviews his / her goal and the steps for accomplishing it. The other group members make suggestions, ask clarifying questions, and generally lend support to the individual's plan to change.

6. Sample goals can be shared voluntarily with the entire group.

Notes to Myself

Step by Step to Action

Goal I Want to Achieve:_____ By This Date: _____

Steps I Must Take	Difficulties I Might Face with Each Step	Resources and People Who Could Help Me Accomplish this Step
1.		
2.		
3.		
4.		
5.		
6.		
7.		

Notes to Myself

Goal Rehearsal to Build Confidence and Skills

Objectives

To provide an opportunity for the participants to review and integrate the ideas and skills presented in the workshop

To help participants imagine themselves successfully reaching a goal as a prelude to achieving it in reality

Group Size

Any size — the exercise is done individually

Time Required

Fifteen to twenty minutes

Physical Setting

Chairs in a circle or comfortable group setting

Materials Utilized

None

Content and Process

The activity begins with a simple relaxation exercise followed by a goal rehearsal. The goal rehearsal process is demonstrated here using a negotiating session as the scenario. The trainer should adapt this format to the topic of his/her session. The material presented here is in dialogue form as the trainer would use it.

Relaxation Exercise

Our work during the past two days has covered many new concepts and skill practice sessions. It will be helpful to you if we take a few minutes now to review and integrate what you have learned. I would like to help you do this through a technique called "goal rehearsal." Goal rehearsal is the process of playing out a situation in your imagination in preparation for successfully handling the situation in the future. There is a good deal of evidence to support the notion that repeated and conscientious mental practice can increase your chances of success under battlefield conditions. I want to show you how goal rehearsal works so that you can use it as part of your preparation for using the skills you have learned in this session.

Let's begin with a simple relaxation exercise as preparation for your goal rehearsal.

1. Make yourself comfortable in your chair. Place your feet flat on the floor. Uncross your arms and legs. Keep your hands open, palms up or down. Close your eyes so that you won't be disturbed.

2. This particular exercise involves "abdominal breathing." This kind of breathing will enable you to oxygenate your blood fully. It is particularly useful when you are under pressure or feeling stressed.

3. Begin by picturing a cat or a dog peacefully asleep in a sunny window. Notice the rhythmic rising and falling of the midsection of this animal. Picture the animal's abdomen rising and falling.

4. Now place your fingertips lightly together across the fleshy part of *your* midsection. Take a breath in such a way that your fingers part slightly when you breathe in. Your fingers part because you are allowing your diaphragm to drop, causing your pelvic organs to protrude slightly. As you breathe out, your fingers should come back together again. In other words as you breathe in, your abdomen will protrude slightly. When you breathe out, your abdomen will drop or retreat slightly toward your spine.

5. Try this now. Think of a balloon alternately filling and emptying. (Trainer: Allow about 2 minutes for them to practice the breathing.)

6. You will use the abdominal breathing exercise before doing the goal rehearsal exercise I am about to describe.

Goal Rehearsal

Now I'm going to take you through a goal rehearsal exercise that you can do in preparation for using the skills you have learned in this workshop. (Trainer: Take this exercise slowly, allowing the appropriate pauses between steps.)

1. Picture your most difficult vendor or other negotiating partner. This is someone with whom you have not been particularly successful in the past. See this person sitting across the table from you. The two of you are having a discussion. (Pause) Now let this picture fade.

2. Now think about an issue or problem you want to negotiate with this person. Think specifically about this issue. (Long pause)

3. Picture yourself carefully preparing. (Pause) Imagine yourself reviewing all of the data and information relevant to this negotiating problem. (Pause) Focus on your main negotiating objective. (Pause) Think of a best alternative for this objective. (Pause) Review in your mind a suitable strategy for achieving this objective. (Pause) Picture yourself preparing thoroughly for this negotiation and feeling secure with your preparation. (Long pause)

4. Now imagine that you are greeting this person. You are friendly, yet business-like as you step into his or her office. (Pause) See yourself talking casually and naturally about your aims for the session to follow. You are optimistic that both of you can come out winners from the discussion. (Long pause)

5. See yourself talking assertively about what you would like to achieve from this discussion. (Pause) Imagine the other party listening receptively. (Pause) Picture yourself asking the other party to describe what he or she would like to get from the discussion. (Pause) Imagine a full discussion of the needs of both parties taking place. (Long pause)

6. Picture yourself identifying those needs where agreement can be reached easily. Picture the other party reacting positively to your observations. (Long pause)

7. Now picture yourself identifying interests that both parties have that are in conflict. (Pause) Imagine the other party beginning to resist your proposals. (Pause) Picture yourself actively listening as the other party raises objections. (Pause) Picture yourself using different kinds of probes to be sure you have heard fully the other party's needs. (Long pause)

8. Imagine yourself saying that some creative problem solving might make it possible for both of you to get what you want. (Pause) See yourself suggesting that each of you contribute some solutions for solving the problem that would meet both of your needs. (Pause) Hear the suggestions from both sides. (Pause) See yourself joining with the other party to pick out the best alternative. (Pause) Picture the other party looking pleased with the results of your discussion. (Pause) Picture yourself feeling good about your results and your strengthened relationship with a heretofore difficult adversary. (Long pause)

Imagine your boss congratulating you for a good job. (Pause)

Open your eyes. What is your reaction to that experience? (Trainer: Ask each participant to describe his/her experience to the group.)

Trainer: Close by suggesting that this kind of goal rehearsal should be part of the preparation process for important negotiations. Practicing three or four times before the negotiation will increase the probability of success.

Sample Handout   A handout similar to the following could be prepared to fit the topic of the session. It serves as a reminder of the steps to follow for a goal rehearsal.

Goal Rehearsal Steps

Directions: Use goal rehearsal techniques to prepare for difficult negotiations. After going through a basic relaxation exercise, have someone read the following eight directions slowly to you as you create mental images of each of them. (Or read these steps into a tape recorder, with pauses, so you can play it back for yourself.) Mentally expand on each of these steps, imagining all of the facets or issues surrounding each step.

1. Picture your most difficult vendor or negotiating partner.

2. Think about your most difficult negotiating issue or problem.

3. Picture yourself carefully preparing for a meeting with this person on this issue.

4. Imagine you are greeting this person.

5. See yourself talking assertively about what you would like to achieve from this discussion. Imagine asking the other party for his/her needs.

6. Picture yourself identifying needs where agreements can be reached.

7. Picture yourself identifying interests that both parties have in conflict.

8. Imagine yourself saying that some creative problem solving might make it possible for both of you to get what you want.

Notes to Myself

2

Sharing Positive Feedback

When participants spend a great deal of time together or frequently interact, the facilitator might want to provide them with the opportunity to share their perceptions of one another. The activities in this chapter help participants to focus on each other and practice giving positive feedback.

Stroke Collection

Objectives   To give participants an opportunity to share positive feedback with one another before parting

Group Size   Up to thirty participants divided into groups of four to six

Time Required   Fifteen minutes

Physical Setting   Tables for four to six; chairs

Materials Utilized   Handout — "Stroke Collection"

Content and Process

1. Prepare a handout like the sample that follows.

2. Indicate that we often neglect to tell others how they helped to make our group experience meaningful.

3. Distribute one copy of the handout per participant and ask them to put their name and date on it.

4. Participants each pass their paper to the person on their right. With a new person's paper in hand, the readers should focus on the group of words listed under "A," decide which of the ten words best describes the person whose name is at the top of the sheet, and circle the word selected.

5. The papers are passed to the right again. The readers select a word from group "B" and follow the same procedure. Continue around the circle until one word from each group has been circled.

6. The papers are then returned to their owners who read and reflect on what others thought of them.

Variations / Comments   To personalize the feedback, "readers" could write their name by the word they circle on each sheet.

Notes to Myself

Stroke Collection

Name _____

Date _____

A.
1. supportive
2. kind
3. attentive
4. cooperative
5. stimulating
6. enthusiastic
7. trustworthy
8. perceptive
9. wise
10. warm

B.
1. reassuring
2. encouraging
3. dependable
4. loyal
5. thoughtful
6. considerate
7. influential
8. affectionate
9. vital
10. tactful

C.
1. zestful
2. helpful
3. accepting
4. refreshing
5. inclusive
6. thorough
7. valuable
8. sensitive
9. ardent
10. creative

D.
1. tender
2. responsible
3. alive
4. steadfast
5. forthright
6. reasonable
7. loving
8. insightful
9. energetic
10. uplifting

E.
1. honest
2. trusting
3. friendly
4. right on
5. deferential
6. positive
7. arousing
8. useful
9. sympathetic
10. aware

F.
1. neat
2. cool
3. delightful
4. empathetic
5. inspiring
6. zealous
7. clever
8. reliable
9. open
10. astute

Notes to Myself

Golden Star Awards

Objectives   To help participants strengthen their relationships within the group

To provide an opportunity for participants to give positive reinforcement to one another

Group Size   Twenty to forty participants; form small groups of four to six participants who have worked together during the workshop

Time Required   Fifteen to twenty minutes

Physical Setting   Tables and chairs

Materials Utilized   One copy of the "Golden Star Award" sheet for each participant; supply of gold stick-on stars; pencils / pens

Content and Process

1. Make some closing comments about the need to take time to personally recognize and appreciate one another.

2. Form small groups of participants who have worked together during the session / workshop.

3. Pass out to each participant a "Golden Star Award" sheet and a supply of stars equal to the number of group members, minus one.

4. Have the participants write their name and enter the date on the appropriate lines on the Award sheet. Then have them pass their Award sheet to the person to their right, who will complete the sentence, "I appreciate you as a member of the team because . . . " The completion of the sentence will be relative to the person whose name is on the sheet. Participants then paste a star in the space to the left of the statement and sign their name to the statement.

5. Have participants continue passing the sheets around the table until each group member has completed the statement for *every* other person in the group.

6. The sheets eventually come around to the owners. Comments can be read silently.

Variations / Comments

- Individual groups can take a few minutes to share their reactions and/or comments on the Award sheet.

- Participants can mingle around the room and share their Golden Star Awards with people from other groups.

- Each person can stand and share with the entire group one of their Golden Star Award statements.

Notes to Myself

Golden Star Awards

Name _____ **Date** _____

"I appreciate you as a member of the team because . . ."

★ 1.

★ 2.

★ 3.

★ 4.

★ 5.

★ 6.

Notes to Myself

Stickers

Objectives   To give participants an opportunity to share positive feedback before parting

Group Size   Up to twenty-five participants per facilitator is best; could be used in small groups of six to eight without a facilitator

Time Required   Fifteen minutes

Physical Setting   Tables and chairs

Materials Utilized   Blank self-adhesive labels (up to 2" square); 8-1/2" x 11" paper

Content and Process

1. Ask the participants to look at the other group members and think about how each person made the experience meaningful to them. Who was particularly helpful? Who provided a useful resource? Who made them laugh?

2. If the group has not already been subdivided, do that now, putting six to eight people in each group. This will ensure that feedback is given equally. Groups can be larger, but it will take more time.

3. Pass out five to seven labels and a sheet of 8-1/2" x 11" paper per person. Participants should write the name of the others in their group at the top of a label and then write one positive comment about that person. (These labels could be signed if desired.) They should write their own name at the top of the piece of paper.

4. Participants stand, take their sheet of paper and prepared labels, and move among their group. They should attach the stickers to each person's sheet. Reinforce the positive feedback by having the giver of the information verbally say the feedback as the label is being attached.

**Variations /
Comments**   Pass the signed sheets of paper around the table. As the
sheets go around, each person should attach the label they
have prepared for the person whose name is on the paper.
When the sheets are returned to the owners feedback can
be verbally reinforced if desired.

Notes to Myself

The Gift

Objectives   To give participants an opportunity to share positive feedback before parting

Group Size   Up to twenty-five participants per facilitator is best; could be used in small groups of eight to ten without a facilitator

Time Required   Fifteen to thirty minutes

Physical Setting   Circle of chairs

Materials Utilized   One gift-wrapped present

Content and Process

1. Form a circle, with or without chairs.

2. Ask the participants to look at the others in the group and to think about what they have given and received from one another. Do this silently.

3. Explain that we often neglect to tell others what they have contributed to a group situation. Ask the participants to focus spontaneously on another person and complete this sentence stem: "Thank you, _____ , for giving me your gift of _____." For example, "Thank you, Sam, for giving me your gift of listening attentively."

4. Start with one person selecting and making his/her comment to another group member. Continue around the circle, one at a time, giving feedback to a different person, until each person has given and received one statement.

5. Next, the participants should think of a "gift" that could be given to each person that would dramatically change some aspect of that person's behavior or life. For example, "I give you, Sally, the gift of laughter to help you survive your new job." As facilitator, start the process, but this time, hand the gift-wrapped package to the receiver as you give the verbal feedback. The person holding the package passes the gift and a new statement to someone else.

Variations / Comments   Sid Simon adds a step to gift giving. He suggests that the participants think of a gift that each of the others in the group could give them to change one or more of their behavior patterns or aspects of their life. Individuals ask for that particular gift or resource from another person. For example, "I would like patience from Lee."

Notes to Myself

Thank You For . . .

Objectives To produce a sense of closure by providing the opportunity for individuals to express their personal appreciation to others in the group for helping them learn during the session

Group Size Any size

Time Required Approximately ten minutes

Physical Setting Open space for people to comfortably mill around without bumping into furniture

Materials Utilized None

Content and Process

1. Ask each participant to think about some positive experience during the session or workshop that is about to end. Each person is to think about one of the others in the group who helped in that experience — helped the participant to learn effectively, to understand a new concept, to practice a new skill, and so forth.

2. Participants then are instructed to stand up and walk over to one of the people they were thinking of and express their appreciation for that person's help in their learning.

3. Bring the group back together for a brief discussion of the benefit of achieving closure through expression of appreciation. Ask individuals to report how they felt when giving and when receiving such appreciation.

Variations / Comments This activity may be combined with other closing activities.

Notes to Myself

We Saw You As . . .

Objectives   To give participants an opportunity to share positive feedback before parting

Group Size   Up to twenty participants

Time Required   Fifteen to thirty minutes

Physical Setting   Circle of chairs

Materials Utilized   None

Content and Process

1. Mention that we often neglect to tell others what we enjoyed or gained from being with them in the group experience. Ask the participants to scan the faces of the other group members, thinking of what they appreciate about each of their peers. Do this silently.

2. Select someone to be the first focus person. Ask some of the others to give positive feedback to him/her. Allow enough time so that the focus person receives at least three comments.

3. Continue around the circle until everyone, including the facilitator, has received some positive feedback.

Variations/ Comments

• Ask that the feedback be focused on how individuals dealt with the workshop topics/issues/skills. For example, in a communication workshop, the feedback could cover how effectively individuals listened to others, spoke in a well organized manner, or worked effectively in small groups.

• Starting with the facilitator, each person states something positive about himself/herself using the sentence stem, "I am proud of the way I _____ during this workshop."

- To provide more anonimity, have participants get in a fully relaxed attitude and position with guided relaxation, lights turned down, and eyes closed. Then name one person and ask for spontaneous feedback on how the others saw that person during the workshop. After several items are mentioned, name a second person to receive feedback. Continue until all participants have been named.

Notes to Myself

Appreciation Circle

Objectives   To provide an opportunity for participants to share some positive feedback

To provide a sense of completion on relationships formed during the group experience

Group Size   Up to twenty participants

Time Required   Approximately two minutes per participant

Physical Setting   Space to form a wide circle of all participants

Materials Utilized   None

Content and Process

1. Explain the purpose and structure of the activity.

2. Have the participants form a large circle, standing about two to three feet apart.

3. Starting with the facilitator, move to face each person, establish eye contact, and express appreciation for what that person contributed during the event. The recipient is instructed to acknowledge the appreciation, but not to respond. When the facilitator is past the first two or three people, the second person begins, and so on. When each person has gone around the circle, they rejoin it at their original place, so that all others who follow can come to face them and express their appreciation.

4. When everyone has gone entirely around the circle, ask for participants to share their appreciation of the group itself. When all volunteers have spoken, announce the close of the event.

Variations / Comments

- The appreciations may be written and handed to each participant as members go around the circle.

- The exchanges can be two-way, allowing reactions to the appreciations by the feedback recipients.

Notes to Myself

Card Line-Up

Objectives   To provide recognition of each participant's positive attributes evidenced during the session

Group Size   Up to twenty

Time Required   Thirty to forty minutes

Physical Setting   Space to line up all the participants shoulder to shoulder from the outer door into the room

Materials Utilized   A deck of 3" x 5" index cards per participant; alphabetized participant list, including facilitator

Content and Process

1. Prepare for each participant a deck of 3" x 5" cards containing enough cards to equal the number of participants plus the facilitator. Prepare an alphabetized participant list (including the facilitator) by last name.

2. Give each person a deck of cards and list of names. Instruct them to write the name of each participant, including themselves and the facilitator, in the upper left corner of a card. Then, write one or two strengths about each person on that card and sign their own name in the lower right corner. On their own card write some of the strengths they think others will write about them. Keep the cards in alphabetical order.

3. Have the participants line up shoulder to shoulder, with the last named person on the list standing at the door and the first person on the list standing at the other end of the line, well into the room.

4. One by one, beginning with the first alphabetized person, they walk down the line and say out loud to the person next in line what they have written about that person on their card. The receiver then says to the

person facing him / her what the receiver wrote about that person and they exchange the cards, putting the cards at the back of their decks so the cards remain in order. Continue on down the line. When the first person has exchanged with two people, the next person should also start down the line and so forth.

5. When the first person gets to the end of the line he / she stands next to the last person, who will be somewhat outside of the room. When the entire group has finished, it will be lined up outside of the room. Each person will now have a deck of cards with positive feedback from their peers. The facilitator then steps out of line and says, "This seminar (workshop, course, etc.) is over."

**Variations /
Comments**

- The facilitator may stay out of the line to help move the activity along.

- The cards could just be exchanged without saying any-thing. This is less personal, however, and takes away from the humorous aspects of the exercise.

- The activity can be done mid-course and processed with the entire group, focusing on predictions and feedback at that point in the group session.

Notes to Myself

3

Giving Prizes, Gifts, and Awards

Giving prizes and gifts to the participants can add a lot of fun to a program. Rather than giving the usual pen or coffee cup, try one of the activities in this chapter for creative ideas and award certificates.

Door Prizes

Objectives To end the group experience on a playful note

Group Size Up to twenty participants (if everyone is to receive a prize); otherwise, any size

Time Required Fifteen to thirty minutes

Physical Setting Chairs facing the front of the room

Materials Utilized Collection of door prizes

Content and Process

1. Depending on how many prizes you want to give, create a list of awards and then think of silly objects that would be appropriate as the door prizes. Gather the door prizes together for later. For example, for the person who . . .

   a. grew the most . . . a ruler
   b. was most patient . . . an egg timer
   c. learned slowly, but surely . . . a turtle
   d. "gave" the most . . . a rubber band
   e. helped us laugh . . . a joke book
   f. is the most tired . . . a pillow
   g. led us in warm-up exercises . . . Richard Simmons pin
   h. helped keep the room neat . . . pins
   i. was outspoken . . . a soapbox
   j. was reflective . . . a mirror

2. Announce that you will end the group experience with some door prizes. Preface each award with comments, creating suspense as to who will receive the award and what it will be.

Variations / Comments

- Form subcommittees of three to five people. Assign each subcommittee the names of three to five other participants. Each committee decides on the award and object to be given and does the actual presentation.

- Ask the participants to give you, the facilitator, an award or two.

- If time or setting does not allow for gathering of actual objects, you could do the exercise verbally.

- Select an item or two such as a book, bookmark, paperweight, or calendar and have a drawing.

Notes to Myself

The Certificate of Participation

Objectives

To give each participant a certificate as a record of participation

Group Size

Up to thirty participants

Time Required

Fifteen minutes

Physical Setting

Chairs facing the front or circle of chairs

Materials Utilized

Certificates

Content and Process

1. Prior to the session prepare a certificate. Some ways to enhance the appearance of the certificate are to:

   a. Keep the content simple.

   b. Include the name and the date(s) of the event.

   c. Include the name of the presenter and the sponsor.

   d. Add a graphic image, emblem, or logo that represents your organization. Examples might include a half-tone outline of your area's skyline, a photograph of your building, or a graphic image from a clip art book.

   e. Select a special paper like parchment or glossy finish.

   f. Add touches to the printed certificate like ribbons, gummed stickers (big stars), or use Chartpak pressure-sensitive graphic tape that comes in many widths and colors.

   g. Enter the participants' names either in calligraphy or with a larger pitch typing element such as Orator. Press-apply letters could also be used.

2. Set the tone for the presentation of the certificates. Make sure you have everyone's attention. Call each person by name and ask him/her to come forward. Hand the certificate to the individual with your left hand, leaving your right hand free for shaking hands. Add a personal comment about each person as you hand him/her the certificate.

Variations/ Comments

- To save time, hand the certificates out as the participants remain seated.

- Encourage a round of applause, either after each award or at the end.

- Combine a small gift with the certificate as a momento of the group experience. You can buy items embossed with your organization or company name. Items you could use include pens, pointers, bookmarks, and paperweights.

Notes to Myself

The Certificate of Appreciation

Objectives   To give each participant a certificate of appreciation from the group

Group Size   Small groups of four to six participants who have worked together during the workshop

Time Required   Thirty minutes

Physical Setting   Any setting

Materials Utilized   Certificates

Content and Process

1. Prior to the session, prepare a certificate. Some ways to enhance the appearance of the certificate are to:

   a. Keep the content simple. Center the phrase "Certificate of Appreciation For."

   b. Include the name and the date(s) of the event.

   c. Include spaces for the names of the group leader and others who are giving or sponsoring the award.

   d. Add a graphic image, emblem, or logo that represents your organization. Use your imagination to think of a graphic that will give this certificate special meaning.

   e. Select a special type of paper such as parchment or glossy finish.

   f. Add touches to the printed certificate like ribbons, gummed stickers, or Chartpak pressure-sensitive graphic tape that comes in many widths and colors.

2. Form small groups of participants who have worked together during the group experience. Explain that each person will be given a certificate of appreciation by their group. Determine who will be the first focus person in each group. Those individuals listen silently as their peers discuss the things for which he / she is appreciated. Once they decide on a single area of

appreciation, that information is carefully penned into the space left on the certificate for that purpose. The focus person now may comment on the category the group selected for him/her.

3. The certificates are given to each person when they are prepared.

4. Rotate the focus person until a certificate is prepared for each person.

Variations / Comments

- Ask the focus persons to leave the room while their certificates are being prepared. Meet with the focus people while they are waiting and discuss what they think they might receive a certificate of appreciation for; what they believe they have contributed to the group's experience; and what they have liked or disliked about the experience. With this variation, hold all certificates until the end when a more formal ceremony can be held.

- Hold the prepared certificates until all are completed. Conduct a ceremony for their awarding, asking the small groups to stand together as each of their members receives their certificate.

- Ask for an award as the facilitator. Leave the room while the entire group prepares your certificate.

Notes to Myself

The Certificate of Self-Appreciation

Objectives To have each participant identify an area in which he/she would like to be appreciated

Group Size Small groups of four to six participants who have worked together during the workshop

Time Required Fifteen minutes

Physical Setting Any setting

Materials Utilized Certificates

Content and Process

1. Prior to the session, prepare a certificate. Some ways to enhance the appearance of the certificate are to:
   a. Keep the content simple. Center the phrase "Certificate of Appreciation For."
   b. Include the name and the dates(s) of the event.
   c. Include spaces for the names of the group leader and of one other participant.
   d. Select a parchment type paper.
   e. Add touches to the printed certificate like ribbons, gummed stickers, or Chartpak pressure-sensitive graphic tape that comes in many widths and colors.

2. Form small groups of participants who have worked together during the group experience.

3. Pass out the certificates. Each participant writes in his/her own name, then thinks of what he/she deserves recognition for while being in this particular group. Examples might include: contributing resources, listening attentively, or willingness to deal with conflict. The area of appreciation is written into the space provided on the certificate.

4. Next, the participants decide from whom they would ideally like to receive this certificate and that individual will be asked to present the award to the recipient.

5. The awards are given in the small groups. Applause is encouraged.

Variations /
Comments

• Hold the prepared certificates until all are completed. Conduct a ceremony for their awarding.

• Give yourself an award as the facilitator.

Notes to Myself

Team Awards

Objectives To provide recognition of each participant's positive attributes evidenced during the event

Group Size Any size; form learning teams of five to six people

Time Required One hour of preparation; one minute per participant for presentation

Physical Setting Tables; chairs

Materials Utilized One Team Award per participant; pens; markers

Content and Process

1. The facilitator should prepare a Team Award sheet like the sample that follows. Set up this closing activity early in the event by assigning a "target team" for each learning team. (For example, Team C will be the "target team" for Team A.) Each learning team is given the assignment of observing the members of its target team for the purpose of presenting a special award to each individual on the target team at the end of the event. Participants are instructed to observe the positive attributes that individual members of their target team display during the event.

2. Remind participants of this assignment from time to time during the event.

3. Toward the end of the event, distribute copies of the Team Award handout. Each member of a learning team will present an award from his/her team to an individual on its assigned target team. This will be done in front of the entire group during the closing activities of the event. The learning teams are to develop their awards through consensus. The award for each person should be neatly completed so it looks special.

4. Have each learning team "number off" its members in the order in which they will present their awards to the members of the target team. Then indicate how the awards will be given across teams. For example, a member from Team A will present Team A's award to a member of Team C. Then a second member of Team A will present the award to a second member of Team C and so forth.

5. Presentations are continued in the order described in step 4 until all learning teams have given their awards to each member of their Target Team. Participants applaud after each presentation.

Variations / Comments

- After each presentation the "awardee" makes a brief statement that begins with: "As a result of attending this event, I intend to . . . "

- Awards can be made within the teams, rather than across them. In this case there are no assignments regarding observing individuals.

Notes to Myself

**Sample
Team
Award**

The _____ Award
(Presenting Team's Name)

For

_____
(Name of Award)

Is Presented to

_____
(Name of Awardee)

In Recognition of His / Her

_____

and _____
(List Two Positive Attributes)

_____   _____

_____   _____

_____   _____

(Team Member Signatures)

* These awards can be embellished with the awarding team's "logo," other artwork, color, etc.

Notes to Myself

4

Coming Home

When participants spend two or more days in a workshop or when the learning experience is intensive, they need a bridge to the "real" world. The activities in this chapter help prepare the participants for their re-entry to work and home life.

The Re-Entry

Objectives   To help participants prepare for their return to work and personal life

Group Size   Any size

Time Required   Ten to fifteen minutes

Physical Setting   Chairs facing the front of the room

Materials Utilized   None

Content and Process

1. The facilitator starts a short lecture with a reference to how the astronauts prepare for their re-entry to earth. It includes what they do while still in space and after they have landed. Remind the participants that they must face re-entry back into their work and personal lives.

2. If the group experience was especially intense, located away from home, or involved several days, the family, friends, and colleagues of the participants will have experienced some isolation, loneliness, perhaps even jealousy. Help the participants to identify what was going on in the lives of their employees, colleagues, or intimates while they were gone.

3. If the group experience was especially meaningful, the tendency will be for individuals to rush home and exclaim, "Oh, you should have been there!" Ask how they have felt when an enthusiastic traveler returned from a trip and made that statement to them.

4. With the participants' help, develop a list of suggestions that will ease their re-entry. Ideas include:

   a. Interview those left behind about what they did while the participant was absent.

b. When asked, "How was your experience?" reply, "I've been exposed to a lot of ideas. Probably the most useful to me was _____. It will take me awhile to finish sorting out the rest." The purpose here is to reduce the tendency to overwhelm the person back home. Instead, relate one idea now and spread out the other ones over time.

c. To a boss say, "You were generous to let me attend this program. I would like to report to you what I have learned. When would be a good time for me to do that?" The purpose here is to establish whether or not the boss wants to hear about the employee's experience. The boss who really wants to hear more will indicate so, which gives the workshop participant a chance to try out new skills and ideas. If it appears that the boss is not really interested, then keep the comments brief.

Notes to Myself

Hi! I'm Home!

Objectives To help participants prepare for their return to work and personal life

Group Size Up to thirty participants

Time Required Thirty to sixty minutes

Physical Setting Some open space

Materials Utilized None

Content and Process

1. Give a short lecture based on information found in the previous activity, "The Re-Entry."

2. Help the participants to identify what was going on in the lives of their employees, colleagues, or intimates while they were in the workshop and the problems they may face upon coming home. Poll them for examples.

3. Roleplay some of the situations they might face. Here are some samples:

    a. The enthusiastic participant who wants to "tell it all" right away.

    b. The participant who finds his/her new ideas falling on "deaf ears."

    c. The participant who faces the resentment or jealousy of a spouse who could not go on this "vacation." The negative feelings could also come from a colleague or employee.

    d. The participant who discovers that his or her employees either did nothing while they were away or "messed up" their work.

    e. The boss who demands a "play-by-play" account of everything the participant did.

Notes to Myself

5

Staying in Touch

The activities in this chapter present ways the participants can stay in touch with one another following the workshop or program. There are suggestions for participants who do and do not live in the same geographic location. One activity shows how to start an on-going support group.

The Name Exchange

Objectives   To ensure that participants know how to contact one another after the workshop

Group Size   Any size

Time Required   Thirty minutes

Physical Setting   Any setting

Materials Utilized   Handout as described below or sheets of paper

Content and Process

1. This activity will need to be done early on the final day so there will be time to have the sheets reproduced (every participant gets a sheet from every other participant). It would be helpful to announce this exercise early in the program so participants can be thinking about their entries.

2. Prepare copies of an information sheet. You could simply provide a paper that has headings for name, address, and phone numbers. However, why not be creative and add a few other headings such as:

   a. "Remember Me As/For": Participants write down what they would like to be remembered for.

   b. "I Need": Write down some resource or area that still needs resolving. Later on another participant may come across an idea or resource that could help the person in need.

   c. "I Can Give": Remind one's peers of resources you can provide. For example, "I can give you information on how to buy a computer."

3. Begin with an explanation of why it can be valuable to stay in touch with one another following the completion of the program. Reasons include: needing to ask for a resource for / from someone in the group; networking to find jobs; seeking information about some organization or person. Ask the participants to suggest other reasons.

4. Allow time for completing the forms.

5. Allow time at the end of the session for participant discussion, if necessary.

Variations / Comments

• A simple way to make sure participants have information about one another is to ask each person to provide some of their business cards to be put on a table where participants can pick up any they want to keep.

• Pertinent information about each person can be typed on a rolodex card. Copies of the cards are printed and distributed to participants.

Notes to Myself

The Postcard

Objectives   To ensure that participants can contact one another

Group Size   Any size

Time Required   Fifteen minutes

Physical Setting   Any setting

Materials Utilized   Supply of postcards (determine how many to allow per participant)

Content and Process

1. Begin with an explanation of why it can be valuable to stay in touch with one another following the completion of the program. Reasons include: needing to ask for a resource for / from someone in the group; networking to find jobs; seeking information about some organization or person; or letting another person know what has been happening to you. Ask the participants to suggest other reasons.

2. Distribute postcards that have been printed or typed on as follows:

> Hi! I thought you'd like to hear what's been happening to me.

3. Ask each person to decide who they would like to keep informed about their progress. Once they decide who will be the recipient(s), allow time for them to get that person(s) to address a postcard.

4. Suggest that the participants put the postcard(s) in their desk calendars approximately one month from the current date as a reminder to mail them.

Variations / Comments

- Leave the postcard blank so participants can send whatever information they choose.

- If your program is held in a hotel or resort, use the stationery or postcards provided by the meeting site.

- Encourage the sending of longer letters.

- Be sure to have some postcards sent to you. Facilitators especially like to hear from participants when they have succeeded in some goal they set during the session.

Notes to Myself

Support Groups

Objectives To help participants develop support groups to meet following the program

Group Size Any size

Time Required Thirty minutes

Physical Setting Tables and chairs for small groups

Materials Utilized List of participants' names, addresses, and phone numbers

Content and Process

1. Explain the value of staying in touch with one another following the completion of the program. Reasons include: needing to ask for a resource from someone in the group; networking to find jobs; getting information about some organization or person; or merely letting another person know what has been happening to you. Ask the participants to suggest other reasons.

2. Explain that a professional support group is "a small group of professionals with a common area of interest, who meet periodically to learn together and to support one another in their ongoing professional development." People meet regularly to share ideas, expand insights, provide practical help to one another, and generally to give support as they try to achieve their goals.

3. Suggest that the participants could form smaller groups based on a common interest. For example: same location, same job, same company, men's or women's groups, special task force, etc.

4. Lead a discussion on how they might like to group themselves. Some individuals may not feel a need to be in a group. Those that live too far apart may form a group and decide how they might stay in touch long distance.

5. Form groups based on the participants' preferences. Review for them some guidelines on how they can organize their group, how often to meet, how to run their group meetings, and how to decide when to disband.

Notes to Myself

6

Saying Goodbye

The activities in this chapter offer quick but pleasant ways to close the session. There are both verbal and nonverbal exercises.

The Closing Circle

Objectives   To give participants an opportunity to "say goodbye" nonverbally

Group Size   Up to twenty participants

Time Required   Fifteen minutes

Physical Setting   Open space with no furniture

Materials Utilized   None

Content and Process

1. Ask the participants to form a circle in the open space.

2. Ask them to scan each face in the circle silently, thinking about their first impressions of each person, what they have learned from each one, and what final words they would like to share with some of them.

3. Allow enough time for the participants to clarify their thoughts.

4. Indicate that it is time to "say goodbye" to one another and to end this experience. Suggest that as they break from the circle, they approach several individuals and say the words they had been thinking about them.

Variations / Comments

• Allow enough time while in the circle to have individuals give feedback to one another.

• Participants may naturally leave the circle and shake others' hands or even give hugs, or you may suggest they do one or the other.

Notes to Myself

The Wiggle Handshake

Objectives To give participants an opportunity to "say goodbye" nonverbally

Group Size Any size

Time Required Fifteen minutes

Physical Setting Open space with no furniture

Materials Utilized None

Content and Process

1. Ask the participants to stand in the open space.

2. State that people often shake hands upon "saying hello" and also upon "saying goodbye." The handshake is a wonderful way to take with you fond memories of the others in the group. However, indicate that you want to show them an innovative way to shake hands.

3. Ask for a volunteer so you can demonstrate the "wiggle handshake."

4. The handshake consists of three actions. First, shake hands normally. Then, without letting go, both people rotate their hands so they can grasp the other person's thumb — shake hands again. Now, release the fingers, but with the thumbs still interlocked, rotate the hands so the palms are facing down, parallel to the floor, with the fingers pointing toward the other person. Now just wave goodbye with your fingers.

5. Be sure they understand the handshake. Announce, "OK, handshakes all around." Participants should circulate and give each other a "wiggle handshake."

Variations / Comments Some participants may not feel comfortable with this playful handshake, so have them give the traditional handshake instead.

Notes to Myself

The Circle Massage

Objectives To give participants an opportunity to "say goodbye" nonverbally

Group Size Up to twenty participants; if more, form smaller groups of ten to fifteen

Time Required Fifteen minutes

Physical Setting Open space with no furniture

Materials Utilized None

Content and Process

1. Ask participants to stand in a circle in the open space.

2. Ask them to scan the faces of those in the circle, to think about what they have gained by being together. Indicate that you are going to give them a chance to thank one another for being here.

3. Have the participants make a quarter turn and move inward until everyone can easily put their hands on the shoulders of the person in front of them. Ask them to give that person a gentle massage. Guide the massage with comments like, "Remember how hard that person worked, so give her a reward for her perserverance," or "Be gentle, he'll be facing a hard world soon enough."

4. After a minute or two, ask them to turn completely around so they are facing the back of the person who just gave them a massage. Remind them that now they will have a chance to really thank someone by giving him/her a thank you massage in return.

5. After a minute, finish the experience either with the group holding hands or hugs all around.

**Variations /
Comments**   In addition to massaging the shoulder and neck area, have participants give a head massage. To keep the head from bobbing, hold one hand firmly on the forehead while the second hand massages the head and neck.

Notes to Myself

Exclamations!

Objectives   To create an enthusiastic, energy-releasing closure to a group session or workshop

Group Size   Any size

Time Required   Three to five minutes

Physical Setting   None

Materials Utilized   None

Content and Process

1. Ask the participants to reflect briefly on their experiences in the session. Ask them to think about how they would sum up that experience.

2. Explain that on a signal everyone is to shout out a word or two that best expresses that person's own feelings about the session.

3. Give the signal — everyone shouts. Then ask everyone to repeat the exclamations when given the signal (or, if they wish, to shout out another expression). Do this several times.

4. Ask everyone to reflect on what they heard. Summarize what you heard and / or ask participants to summarize what they heard being said.

Variations / Comments

- Step 4 is optional; the session can be ended at Step 3.
- This exercise is similar to the current boxed game called "Outburst."

Notes to Myself

Final Words

Objectives   To provide participants with a sense of closure while giving feedback on the session

Group Size   Any size

Time Required   Reserve the final five minutes of the session for this activity

Physical Setting   Blank wall space by the doors

Materials Utilized   Water-based marking pens (permanent ink types may go through the paper and mar the walls); newsprint

Content and Process

1. Some time prior to the activity, post large sheets of blank newsprint by the door or the doors through which the participants will leave. The larger the group size, the more sheets will be needed. Use one large sheet for every ten participants.

2. Conclude the session, leaving a few minutes for this final activity.

3. Explain to the group members that the newsprint paper has been posted to receive their closing comments. As they leave, participants are invited to write a word, or a few words, on the paper, expressing their feelings at the close of the session. This gives them a chance to leave behind some final comments about their experience.

Variations / Comments   The group leader may wish to model the activity by going to the newsprint and writing his or her own brief comment.

Notes to Myself

Let's Sing!

Objectives   To give participants an opportunity to "say goodbye" through music

Group Size   Any size

Time Required   Depends on songs selected

Physical Setting   Large circle, sitting or standing

Materials Utilized   Song sheets

Content and Process

1. Select appropriate songs that are positive and happy. You can get ideas by visiting your local music store. Some suggestions are:

   a. "We've Only Just Begun"
   b. "Happy Days Are Here Again"
   c. "Smiles"
   d. "What a Wonderful World"
   e. "So Long, Farewell"
   f. "So Long, it's Been Good to Know You"
   g. "Put a Little Love In Your Heart"
   h. "I'd Like to Teach the World to Sing"
   i. "Climb Every Mountain"
   j. "Take the Moment"
   k. "Til We Meet Again"
   l. "On My Journey"
   m. "Rolling Home"

   You may want to alter or adapt the lyrics to your workshop topic.

2. Type up a song sheet and prepare a copy for each participant.

3. The activity will be enhanced if you have someone available to play the piano or guitar.

4. State that songs are often a pleasant way to "say goodbye" at the end of a workshop experience.

5. Pass out the song sheets. Ask everyone to enter in with cheerful voices and sing together. The trainer or person selected should lead the group in singing.

Notes to Myself

7

Following Up

Facilitators often fail to follow up with the participants. The activities in this chapter will offer some ways to do that. Included are ways to offer additional suggestions to the participants or to reinforce what was presented in the workshop.

You'll Be Hearing from Me

Objectives   To ensure that participants have follow-up contact with the facilitator

Group Size   Any size

Time Required   Depends on the method selected

Physical Setting   None

Materials Utilized   Depends on the method selected

Content and Process

1. As you plan your workshop design, review the following methods that can be used to follow up with the participants:

   a. Send a questionnaire to help the participants identify the areas they still need to develop.

   b. Send another copy of the workshop evaluation to determine what has been retained.

   c. Add them to your mailing list so they will receive your newsletter or other resources.

   d. Give them a subscription to a magazine or newsletter service that prints your name on it.

   e. Give them your phone number and encourage them to call you.

   f. Call them to see if they have any problems or to invite them to another workshop.

   g. Plan a reunion of their group.

2. At the end of your workshop, let them know which method(s) you will use to stay in touch with them.

Variations / Comments   Have the group help you decide which of these methods would best meet their needs.

Notes to Myself

Success is Up to You!

Objectives To provide a list of ways participants can ensure that they retain what was learned in the workshop

Group Size Any size

Time Required Depends on method and number of participants

Physical Setting None

Materials Utilized Handout; list of participants' names and addresses

Content and Process

1. Prepare a handout similar to the one that follows. You can add the name of the workshop and / or the name of your organization.

2. Within two weeks of the workshop, prepare and send a letter that expresses your appreciation of their participation in your program. Refer to the purpose of the handout you are enclosing and the importance of follow-up activities that will ensure retention of what they have learned.

Variations / Comments Distribute the handout at the end of your workshop and have participants make a commitment to doing one of the suggestions listed.

Notes to Myself

Success is Up to You!

You have successfully completed a _____ workshop and learned a lot. But, you know how easily your good intentions to apply what you have learned can get lost in the hubbub of everyday life.

Did you know that it takes a minimum of thirty days to change a behavior, kick a habit, or integrate a skill? It has been proven that you will get results only if you consistently practice the change you desire.

Here is a list of suggestions that will help you put your most important goals into action.

You cannot afford to merely let things happen;
If you seek success, you will have to make things happen!

1. Review your notes, the handouts, and your action plan within twenty-four hours of the workshop, or at least periodically. Update your action plan.

2. Write a "Dear Boss" thank-you letter expressing appreciation for the time and money invested in your professional development. Also review the three key ideas you learned and determine how your boss might help you succeed in putting your ideas to work.

3. Over coffee or lunch, tell your boss about this workshop and how you plan to put some of the ideas into action. Again, give your thanks and ask for your boss' assistance.

4. Give to your staff, colleagues, family, or friends an "executive summary" of the best three ideas or skills you learned. This helps to clarify and reinforce what you have learned.

5. Write your primary goal on a 3" x 5" card or a "Post-It" and place it in a conspicuous location in your car, at home, and at work.

6. Keep a daily or weekly log to track your progress in achieving your plan of action.

7. Locate an additional resource to aid you in reaching your goal: book, tape, article, or another workshop.

8. Contact another participant from the workshop within two to three weeks. Check on one another's progress and application of what you each learned.

9. Start a support group for yourself and others who are trying to reach common goals.

No horse gets anywhere until he is harnessed.
No steam ever drives a machine until it is confined.
No river is ever turned into electrical power until it is tunneled.
No life ever grows great until it is focused, dedicated, and disciplined.

Notes to Myself

A Letter to Myself

Objectives   To reinforce what was learned in the program

To renew determination to reach set goals

Group Size   Any size

Time Required   Ten minutes

Physical Setting   Any setting

Materials Utilized   Stationery and an envelope for each participant

Content and Process

1. Have participants address an envelope to themselves.

2. Ask them to write a letter to themselves about the changes they want to make as a result of what they have learned. They should also include their most important goal.

3. Have them put their letter in the envelope and seal it.

4. Collect the letters and mail them to the participants thirty days after the program ends.

Notes to Myself

Acknowledgments

I would like to give credit to the following people for their contributions to this collection of exercises. My special thanks go to Rollin Glaser, Christine Glaser, Barbara Roadcap, Marshall Sashkin, and John Jones for their efforts in preparing this second edition.

Chapter One

Reflect and Share
Dr. Sidney Simon

My Personal Learning Goal
Rollin Glaser

I Learned and Plan To . . .
Dr. Jerry Weinstein

Goal Rehearsal to Build Confidence and Skills
Rollin Glaser

Chapter Two

Golden Star Awards
Rollin Glaser

The Gift
Dr. Sidney Simon

Thank You For . . .
Dr. Marshall Sashkin

Appreciation Circle
Dr. John E. Jones

Card Line-Up
Dr. John E. Jones

Chapter Three

Team Awards
Dr. John E. Jones

Chapter Six

The Wiggle Handshake
Dr. Joel Goodman

The Circle Massage
Dr. Sidney Simon

Exclamations!
Dr. Marshall Sashkin

Final Words
Dr. Marshall Sashkin

Chapter Seven

A Letter to Myself
Rollin Glaser